Table of Contents

An Employment Contract is a document which contains conditions of employment with employees and contractors like start date, salary offered, benefits, termination clauses, payment terms etc. It is very important to have written contract in place to avoid any ambiguity in service conditions or benefits offered. Below figure outlines various types of contracts in US.

1. **Full Time Employment Contracts**

(With Benefits)

2. **1099 Contract**
3. **Corp to Corp Contract**
4. **W2 Hourly Contract**

Full Time Employment Contracts

Nothing in the universe is constant except change. Entropy and randomness would really look beautiful if someone is receptive to change.

Full time employment contracts give slightly better sense of security to the potential candidates applying for prospective jobs and to the employees already working within the organization. Most of the employers have employment at will contracts and either employees or employers can give 2 weeks written notice OR payments in lieu of notice and terminate the employment contract. In full time employment; employees generally get the benefits along with the salary. The termination clause is generally mentioned in the contract. It may be more than 2 weeks for both the parties if mutually agreed upon and generally employment is at will.

Some of the features that definitely distinguish full time employees from contractors are better sense of belonging, being part of performance appraisals, employment engagement surveys (some companies do involve contract work to participate in such surveys), and reporting structure.

Employer is responsible to deduct Social security, Medicare and income tax (state and federal taxes) from employee's salary and issue a W4 at the end of Tax year. Employer also pays the Social security, Medicare and Federal unemployment taxes (FUTA) to the government. It is employee's responsibility to file state and federal tax returns every year. Employee files the taxes using his / her social security number

Employer Benefits – Full Time Employment

Employer Benefits – Full Time Employment

Full time employees are generally entitled to benefits. These benefits are governed by organization's HR policies. Some of the benefits generally offered by the employers are discussed below

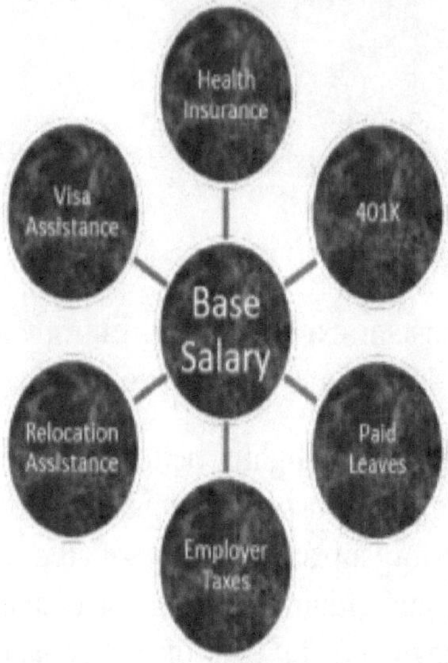

Full time employees are generally entitled to benefits. These benefits are governed by organization's HR policies. Some of the benefits generally offered by the employers are discussed below

Visa Assistance Although most organizations prefer to hire locally in US however in case if the required skill is not available in local market then organizations As part of business plan ; Organizations see the growth and sales pipelines and plan the number of H1-B / L1 visa application sponsorships for the current and next year. Local hiring of Green card holders and US Citizens is fairly simple. However in case the candidate is on H1-B visa then filing of a transfer petition with USCIS is needed. (H1-B Visa transfer).If organizations plan to transfer employee from India or other offshore location then they choose Visa ready (H1/ L1) internal employees and send them on overseas assignment to United States. This incurs cost which is borne by the organizations and part of employer benefit.

Paid Leaves

Most Employers provide 2 weeks of paid leaves and US national holidays as part of paid days to promote a healthy work - life balance. For other employers it may vary one example – employees getting transferred from another country to US may get additional 3-5 days off as part of relocation assistance so that employee settles in at new location and country. Another example – some employers can add tenure to paid leaves as part of retention program where employees tenured 10 year or above get additional 2 days or similar programs. Please refer to benefits section for more details.

Fair labor Standards Act (FLSA) does not mandate an employer to pay for sick leaves, maternity leave or other health related absence from work. Under FMLA act, eligible employees can take 12 weeks of unpaid leaves for maternity, child adoption or serious health conditions

Federal law does not mandate employers to pay for time actually not worked by employees including Jury duty leaves. However some of the state's law does mandate employers to pay for jury duty
Paid Leave is part of organizations corporate policy and different employers make have higher or lower paid leaves than standard 2 weeks.

401K Savings Plan

In United States, 401K is tax benefit/ Tax qualified and defined pension account. Employees can contribute set amount or salary percentage to contribute towards 401K funds. Generally 401K contributions are excluded from employee's taxable income. Employers can contribute to employees' accounts; however employer's contribution purely depends on organizational policy and law does not mandate companies to contribute towards 401K plan. Employees cannot keep retirement funds in their account indefinitely. They have to start taking withdrawals from your IRA, or retirement plan account when they reach age of 70½ years.
401K is a good recruitment and retention tool for employers.

Employee contributions

Employees can contribute up to $12,500 to a SIMPLE IRA plan If they are under the age of 50 years, Employees can contribute an additional $3,000 (in 2015 and 2016) in catch-up contributions if they are over the age of 50 years. The maximum yearly limit for employee contribution / deferral in the 401k plan is governed by the IRS specified for the plan year. Employees have a choice of investing their salary deferrals in different varieties of mutual funds. Employers may or may not provide a matching contribution.

EMPLOYER & EMPLOYEE TAXES

FICA (employee and employer)

Federal Insurance Contributions Act (FICA) is a US federal tax on payroll which is applicable or imposed on both employer and employee for the funding of Social security and Medicare. Rate of FICA tax withholdings for employees and employers (employer and Employee, Both)
Social Security's Old-Age, Survivors, and Disability Insurance (OASDI) Taxes: 6.2 %
Medicare's Hospital Insurance (HI) Taxes: 1.45 %
Total: 6.2% + 1.45% = 7.65 % for Employer + 7.65 % for Employee (for employees, this is in addition to applicable federal income tax and applicable state taxes)

FUTA (Employer only)

The Base wage for Federal unemployment tax is $7,000. Once employee year to date salaries exceed $7,000 then employer stops paying FUTA for that particular employee. The maximum tax paid by the employer is $420 per employee per year and the minimum tax is $42 per employee per year

Employee Tax Responsibility

Employee Tax withholding – done by employer and deposited to respective tax authorities.

Medicare Tax + Federal Income Tax + Social Security Tax = Total Employee Tax Liability

Employer Tax Responsibilities

FUTA (Federal/State Unemployment Tax) + Social Security Tax + Medicare Tax = Total Employer Tax Responsibilities

Conversion: full time salary to equivalent hourly cost:

Lot of candidates and recruiters multiply the hourly rate to 40 hours a week times 52 weeks which is unfair to convert the hourly rate into equivalent yearly salary with benefits. Below table shows yearly salary with benefits and its equivalent hourly cost.

For Example: Yearly salary of $100,000 will incur the cost of approximately $66/hour to the organization or in other words paying a 1099 contactor $66 per hour is equivalent to paying an employee $100,000 per year from cost perspective.

Employer taxes are 7.65 % of base salary and additional payroll accounting cost, for ease of calculation   it is taken as 9% of base salary.

Health Insurance cost

The Health insurance benefits differ for various companies and employee contributions towards health insurance also differ per organizations policy. The average insurance cost is taken as $600 per month per employee for calculations ($600 X 12 months = $7200). This cost to the company can be higher or lower depending upon the insurance plan.

Cost of Paid Leaves/Year

Paid leaves cost is calculated for standard 2 weeks of paid time off Plus 1 week national holidays. The cost of paid leaves is 3 weeks salary.

Example at $100,000 per year salary, per week salary = $100,000/52 weeks = $1923

3 weeks salary is $1923 X 3 = $5769

Cost of 401K

401K cost is calculated at matching contribution for initial 8 % of the salary. Example if an employee contributes $8000 per year into 401K account; employer matches equal contribution of $8000 into 401K account. This can be higher or lower depending upon organization's Human resource policies.

Total cost is calculated by adding all the recurring costs (A+B+C+D+E)

Salary cost versus overall cost of the resource

The below table does not include any administrative costs, one time relocation cost and Visa sponsorship cost if applicable. If a company sends an employee from offshore to US on H1 or L1 visa; the over cost will be slightly higher than calculated below.

You can see in the below pie chart; the additional cost on account of benefit is approx. 26% in addition to the salary. In general the cost of benefits may range between 25 % to 30% of the base salary offered. It may be higher for employers providing great benefits to employees.

Cost of Benefits as percentage of Salary

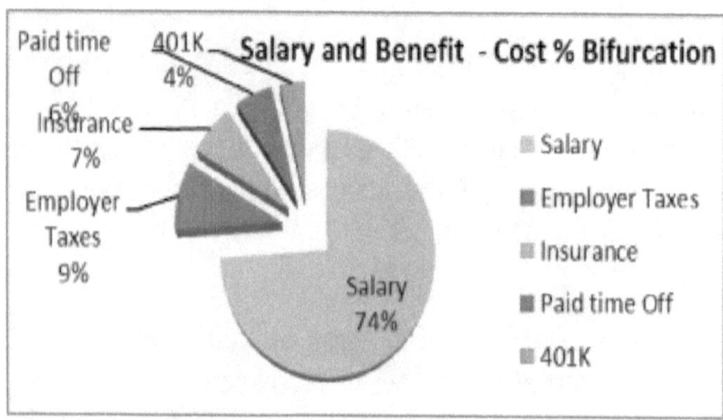

Hourly cost equivalent

Hourly cost equivalent is calculated by dividing the total cost by 1960. Out of 5 weeks per year, 3 weeks are taken off on the account of paid time off. (49 weeks

X 40 hours per week = 1960 hours)

Example: At yearly salary of $100,000, the hourly cost equivalent is total cost: $129969 / 1960 = $66.3 rounded off to $66 per hour. These are guidelines and hourly cost may be slightly higher or lower than the figures shows depending upon the benefits offered by the organizations.

This may give a fair insight to Recruiters and Sales & HR professionals on offering equivalent salary to certain hourly rate to maintain the expected margins for the organization. Example if a contractor first asks for $50/hour on 1099 and after that he/she asks what is the full time salary (with benefits) the you can calculate the salary equivalent. Similar if a contractor is asking for $50/hr (cost will be approx. $54/hour including employer taxes), recruiters can find the equivalent salary

Hourly to Hourly Rate: Cost Equivalent calculation at various salary levels

Base salary/Year	(SSN, Medicare/FUTA, FICA Taxes)	Health Insurance Cost	Cost of Paid Leaves	Cost of 401K/Year	Total Cost/Year	Hourly Equivalent Cost
40000	3150	7200	2019	2800	50169	26
45000	3600	7200	2308	3200	56308	29
50000	4050	7200	2596	3600	62446	32
55000	4500	7200	2885	4000	68585	35
60000	4950	7200	3173	4400	74723	38
65000	5400	7200	3462	4800	80862	41
70000	5850	7200	3750	5200	87000	44
75000	6300	7200	4038	5600	93138	48
80000	6750	7200	4327	6000	99277	51
85000	7200	7200	4615	6400	105415	54
90000	7650	7200	4904	6800	111554	57
92500	8100	7200	5192	7200	117692	60
95000	8325	7200	5337	7400	120762	62
97500	8550	7200	5481	7600	123831	63
100000	8775	7200	5625	7800	126900	65
105000	9000	7200	5769	8000	129969	66
110000	9450	7200	6058	8400	136108	69
115000	9900	7200	6346	8800	142246	73
120000	10350	7200	6635	9200	148385	76
125000	10800	7200	6923	9600	154523	79
130000	11250	7200	7212	10000	160662	82
135000	11700	7200	7500	10400	166800	85
140000	12150	7200	7788	10800	172938	88
145000	12600	7200	8077	11200	179077	91
150000	13050	7200	8365	11600	185215	94
155000	13500	7200	8654	12000	191354	98
	13950	7200	8942	12400	197492	101

Relocation Assistance

Relocation assistance or relocation benefits can vary for different organizations. Some of the widely offered benefits are flight tickets from initial location to work city or work location for self and immediately family, airport transfers, initial hotel stay for couple of weeks.

Lease breakage if applicable and airport transfers / car rentals for couple of weeks. Some of the employers do offer some joining bonus or retention bonus and promise to sponsor green card after mutually agreed upon time frame if the new hire is on H1-B visa.

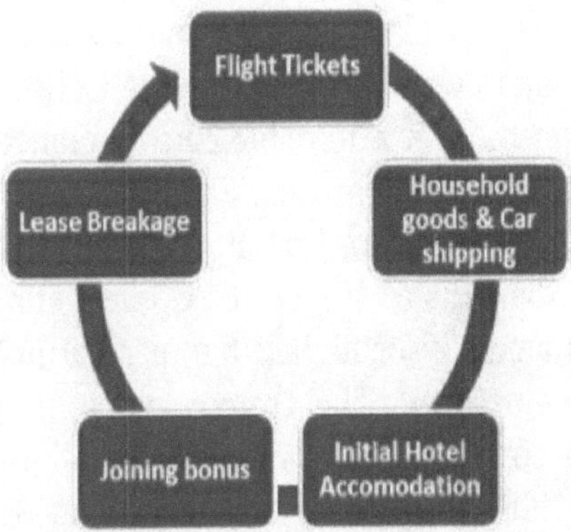

If the organization or the specific position does not offer relocation assistance; generally the job posting or the recruiters make it clear during the initial hiring process that relocation assistance is available or not. Relocation assistance must be discussed and put in writing with the potential candidate to avoid any confusion after the hiring is done and candidate has joined the organization.

International Relocations

Intra – Company transfer of employees from India and other offshore locations to US involves additional activities like briefing & inducting the employees on US culture and immigration process, setting role expectations because the employees will be client facing and they represent the company in front of the customers.

Health Insurance

Most of the organizations offer employer sponsored Health insurance benefits to employees and their immediate family (Spouse and Child/ Children). The benefits can vary in quality and therefore the cost of the health insurance also varies. Higher the insurance premium correlated to good insurance plan.

In addition to medical insurance, most of the employers offer optional dental and Vision insurance and employer sponsored Short term disability (STD), Long term disability (LTD) and life insurance

Higher the coinsurance and lower the deductibles / Out of pocket maximum, better the plan

Affordable care Act (ACA) or Obamacare in short. ACA act was President Barack Obama in 2010 and upheld by the Supreme Court on June 28, 2012. ACA mandates employer to offer affordable care insurance to Full time and Contract W2 employees. 1099 contractors, Corp to Corp (C2C) contractors and Independent Corp to Corp contractors are exempt i.e. employers are not mandated to offer ACA benefits to 1099 or C2C contractors. If an employee makes at least $45,960 annually or higher; the medical insurance premiums can be 100% paid by employee. The current cap is maximum 9.5 % of employee's salary to be contributed towards ACA premiums. If an employee makes below $45,960; then employer must contribute towards the ACA premiums. ACA is a great initiate to cover maximum number of people under health insurance plan at an affordable cost.

In the below example the 90% coinsurance with less Out of pocket is a better plan 70% coinsurance. The overall cost of better plan will be higher. Some organizations offer excellent health insurance benefits where as other may not. It is a good idea for Candidates to compare the health insurance plans for different companies when they make a decision to join an organization.

W2 Contract Employment

W2 contract employment is more or less same as full time employment contract a far as tax treatment of salary is concerned. In W2 employment contract employee deducted state and federal income taxes and pay employer portion of Social security and Medicare taxes and additional federal unemployment taxes. Employee files the taxes using his / her social security number

Major difference from full time employment contract is that on W2 contract the salary is paid on hourly basis which is based on number of hours worked which is generally 40 hours a week. Another major difference from full time employment contract is on W2 contract – employees generally do not get the benefits unless otherwise specified in the offer contract.

Under Affordable care act (Obamacare) which is recent law passed in US mandates employers to provide an option of affordable care to W2 contract employees and Full time employees

As far as employer cost is concerned – it is between 8 to 9 % or higher on top of hourly salary / hourly pay rates paid to employees accounted for employer taxes (Social security, Medicare and federal unemployment or FUTA taxes) and administration fee.

Some employers prefer to hire Contract employees considering future business contingencies and business risks and do not want to deal with full time employee layoffs in an event business suffers a major loss or contract employee becomes redundant in rapidly changing business environment. On the other hand some candidate / potential employees also prefer contract employment as they may be covered in health insurance from spouse's employer and do not want to contribute any money towards health insurance OR they simply prefer number of hours worked in a week multiplied by hourly rate straight into the bank account.

Companies may hire W2 contract employee's on their own payroll or through some of the preferred vendors. In case of vendor arrangement; the liability to pay the salary and tax deduction along with hire and fire rights remain with the vendors.

Non-compete is mutually agreed with employer and vendor where employers / customers can directly hire the candidates without any waiting period of separation of candidate employment with vendor OR this may have 6-12 months' notice period OR vendor may / may not charge such employment conversions with employers / customers

Separation clause is generally 2 weeks written notice from either parties or payments in case of no notice served OR otherwise as specified in the written employment contract

1099 Contract

1099 contracts are nonexclusive means Independent contractor can work for different clients in the same time period. He /she file his own taxes. They are flexible in their schedule and do not get benefits from the employer

From the cost perspective, cost to employer is same as the pay rate. Example if an employer pays $40/hour to an Independent contractor or 1099 contractor, the cost to employer remains 40/hr because it is the responsibility of contractors to file taxes and pay the taxes.

Generally 1099 contracts are non-exclusive i.e. a 1099 contractor can work with multiple customers at any given point of time. The main difference between a 1099 contractor and an independent Corp to Corp contractor is; a 1099 contractor pays his / her taxes against his Social Security number where an independent Corp to Corp contractor pays his / her taxes against Employer Identification Number (EIN) or Tax identification Number

Guidelines on IRS 20 point checklist to determine the 1099 Independent contract status

1. Investment: worker has made investment in the equipment and facilities used to do the work? Phone, Office, Internet, Laptop etc (The greater the investment by worker, more likely chances of worker being independent contractor.)

2. Does worker Works for more than one Company / Organization: Does the worker work for more than one company at any time? (This tends to indicate independent contractor status, most full time employee may have clause of exclusivity in their employment contract

3. Instructions. Organization has the right to give the worker instructions about when, where, and how to work? (This shows the control over the person.)

4. Training. Does the organization train the worker to do his / her job in a specific manner or way? (Independent contractors are trained and don't expect the training.)

5. Integration. How important is the worker for your organization. IS he/ she an important and integral part of the business? (This may show that the worker is subject to organization's control.)

6. Services Offered: Should the worker provide the services personally, as opposed

to delegating tasks to someone else? (Independent contractor can perform the services personally or through an agent.)

7. Assistants. Independent contractors can hire and pay their own staff or agents

8. Continuing relationship- continuing or long lasting relationship indicate employee status.

9. Work hours: Independent contractors set their own working hours and schedules

10. Fulltime work. Independent contracts are nonexclusive and not necessarily 40 hours a week

11. Is the work performed on company premises? Independent contractors can perform the work on premises or off premises

12. Is the individual required to follow a set of sequence or defined routine to perform his work?(no for Independent contractors)

13. Work Reports. Should the individual give you reports regarding his/her work?(no for Independent contractors)

14. Pay Schedules: Is the individual paid by the hour, week, or monthly? (Independent contractors are generally paid by the Task or job, although the industry practice they may be paid per hour

15. Expenses. Business or Travel expenses reimbursed? (no for Independent contractors)

16. Business partnership: Is the individual free from incurring a loss or gaining profit based on his work? ?(no for Independent contractors)

17. Tools and materials: Dos the company supply individual with needed tools or materials?

(Independent contractors generally use their own tools and Equipment's.)

18. Does the individual limit the availability of his services to the general public?

19. Right to fire .Can you fire the worker?

20. Can the individual terminate his services at any time?

Many employers prefer not to do 1099 contracts. Reason being millions of dollars of tax money may be lost by IRS if 1099 contracts don't file the taxes correctly in a timely manner. Organizations are   not mandated to withhold any taxes at source for 1099 contractors.

If the contractor wants to work as independent contractors, the better choice for employers and recruiters is to ask if they are incorporated and if they can share the Employer Identification number? If they are incorporated, it's better to extend an independent Corp to Corp contract to them instead of 1099 contracts.

Independent Corp to Corp contracts are similar to regular Corp to Corp contracts except generally the contractors is the only employee of the corporation in Independent Corp to Corp contracts

In terms of Cost, Independent Corp to Corp contracts and 1099 both have same cost implications for the company i.e. paying $50 / hour on 1099 and paying paying $50 / hour – both the cases the cost to the company (client) remains $50/hr

Cost Comparison between Various contracts

Item	W2 Contract (without Benefits)	1099 Contract	Corp to Corp Contract	Independent Corp to Corp Contract
Hourly Rate	$50/Hour	$50/Hour	$50/Hour	$50/Hour
Cost to the company (Client)	$54.5/Hour	$50/Hour	$50/Hour	$50/Hour

CORP TO CORP CONTRACTS

Corp to Corp is a contract between two corporations (corporation to corporation).

Quite often; the body shopping companies marketing / selling their candidates in IT industry will always ask for this type of contract. The candidates these companies or organizations market (Popularly known as "bench sales") are generally on H1-B visas; however these companies can market Green card holders or US citizens as well.

From cost perspective, if company A is into Corp to Corp contract for a particular skill- example – Java developer with Company B (provider or Consultant or candidate) and agrees to pay for example $58 per hour to company B. In this case the cost of candidate for company A remains $58 per hour as payment of salary or other expenses are the responsibility of company B

It is responsibility of company B to pay salary or hourly rate and pay the employer taxes to US tax authorities and deduct appropriate Federal / state taxes from employee's pay cheque.

At times; you may be surprised to know that there are no many vendors / companies involved in supply of 1 candidate.

Thumb rule is lower the number of companies involved (layers); lower will be the cost of candidate to the final client. Additional in less number of layers, candidate also gets the benefits of higher salary / hourly rate.

Payment terms on Corp to Corp contracts are generally net 30 which means primary vendor is responsible to make the payments within 30 days after invoice is received. Some companies may have net 15 or net 45 days of payment term.

Example of payments on a net 30 payment terms on Corp to Corp Contracts

Example of Corp to Corp Candidate flow and layers

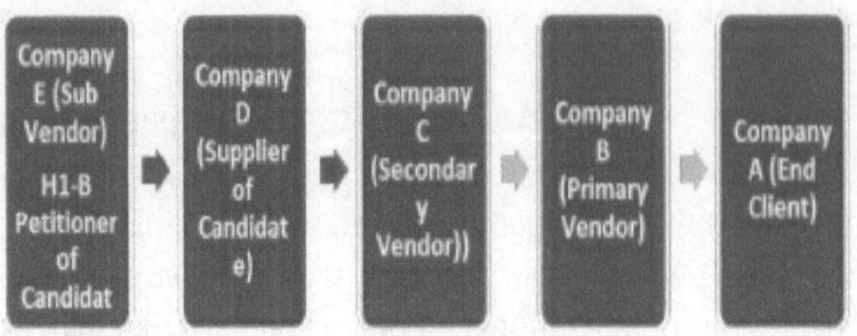

Non Solicitation Clause & Notice Period on Corp to Corp Contracts

You can refer to the above example where a Candidate / Contractor work through multiple layers. Generally the Corp to Corp contracts have Non Solicitation Clause in the contract or purchase order which mean that candidate cannot join break the layers. In above example candidate on payroll of company E cannot join Company D.

Further if the contract specified that candidate cannot join primary vendor or customer then candidate may not join either A, B or C organizations. Non Solicitation Clauses have for 6 or 12 months of cool off period generally (unless clause states other cool off period); i.e. After contract completion, same candidate can be hired by either A, B, C or D Organization.

Some primary vendors or end customers will have written contract to hire clause to hire the contractor after initial 6 or 12 months and where such clause is specified in the contract, Primary vendor, secondary vendor or client can directly hire the contractor without any cool off period.

Contract termination notice period is generally 2 weeks of written notice with or without reason (unless contract has a different kind of notice period) or payments in absence of specified notice served. Based upon business contingences; Primary vendor, secondary vendor or customer can terminate the contract before the specified period by giving 2 weeks written notice.

Resume Inflation & Fake Profiles in Corp To Corp Bench Sales

A software developer with 2 + years of experience will demand certain salary and another candidate with 8+ years of experience with demand certainly higher salary based upon skill and experiences.

Some of the companies selling candidate bench may fake the resumes and inflate the experience from actual or no experience to 4 or 6 or even 8+ years of experience. At times; it may be frustrating & embarrassing for recruiters to face customer escalations at such cases.

Example of Resume Inflation (Fake Resume)

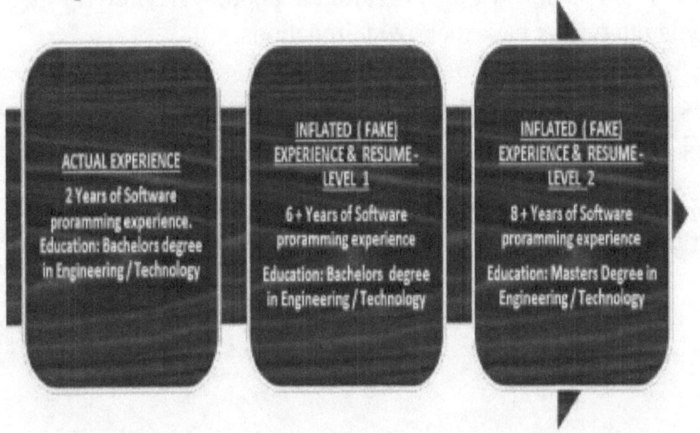

In the above diagram, the Level 1 fake / inflated resume may be marketed for average candidates. Level 2 fake / inflated resume may be presented or marketed for above average or good candidates.

There can be various reasons for this malpractice in IT industry. Some of them may be as follows:

<u>Vendor / employer intends to make more money and therefore fake the resume to get higher billing rates</u>

<u>Vendor/ employer intend to market non-qualified candidates for skilled IT positions and make money.</u>

<u>Vendor/ employer intends to increase the probability and chance of their candidate selection</u>

If there is gap in IT Demand and supply and required skill is not available in the local market, Vendor/ employer intends to fake the non IT profiles and position them to clients or primary vendors.

Finally if the fake / inflated candidates cracks the interview then bingo! Otherwise organizations can misrepresent the candidates – example resume of candidate A is shared with customer and interview is given by candidate B (another candidate) and after selection, candidate A joins the customer. There is huge risk involved in these examples not only in terms of financials; however in terms of integrity and customer Trust. No wonder many clients expect face to face interviews to avoid such situations or at least conduct video conference / skype interviews after initial phone screening. Video conference / skype interviews have their own limitations.

Flowchart Diagram –Example of Fake candidate joining

Screening and initial Checks to screen out Inflated / Fake candidate Profiles

Some of the basic screening questions can help talent acquisition professionals to avoid sharing fake candidates with clients.

    a. Ask general questions about candidate's education, year in which he/she completed his / her degree and try to validate the years of experience with age and see if a 24 years you graduate is claiming that he/she has 6 + years of experience then it is a red flag.

    b. Ask questions about the cities candidates have mentioned to work. Example if a candidate has mentioned that he/she worked at Tampa, Florida then you may ask questions on weather, office commute and basics of project they worked on.

    c. Was it a team effort or individual contributor role?

    d. Always take 1-2 professional references from last 2-3 projects for short term projects and validate the references.

    e. You may like to ask for a valid US photo identification to validate the name

    f. Ask for a valid Vis copy or 797 if the candidate or his/her employee claims to be on H1-b visa status. You can visit https://egov.uscis.gov to check the validity of the visa

g. You can check the candidate's departure / arrival – I94 records at https://i94.cbp.dhs.gov/I94/consent.html to validate the authenticity of experience shown in the United States.

h. Face to face interviews are best; else insist on initial Video or Skype screening

i. Have a written anti- fraud clause in the Corp to Corp contract or purchase order

j. If a vendor is submitting sharing a Green card holder or US citizen then ask the candidate why he/she is being represented by a recruiting agency instead of them speaking with the recruiters directly without involvement of vendors. The generic answer of having a commitment is too cozy a trap to believe in.

k. Post selection and candidate joining; talk to the candidate to validate that the candidates who joined and candidate who was interviewed are same.

Background Checks

Most employers conduct a background check post offer to ensure that the information candidate supplied during the interview process is genuine. Some companies conduct basic background checks however other organizations especially in Airlines, defense or financial industries. A written consent from the candidate must be taken in advance before initiating the pre-employment background investigations. It is illegal to discriminate against any potential candidate based on their age, gender, or sexual orientation, color, ethnicity or country of origin

SSN Trace

Social Security number trace reports the details like date when & where the SS# was issued, first and last name associated with SS#, address associated with specific SS#. Employers can also get the details if the Social security number supplied is valid or invalid.

Employment Verification

Most employers conduct either employer verification for last two employers or employer verification for last 5 or 10 years. Details like position held, salary data and employment dates may be verified

Education Verification

Employers conduct Verification of education either from the colleges or institutes or validation of degree certificates supplied by the candidates. This may include certification of education details internationally if the bachelor's degree is completed outside of US.

Criminal Investigations: Criminal Investigations are very important to ensure that the candidate is free of criminal background. These include regional & national sex offenders, Court Searches, Wants and warrants, US – Nationwide Federal Nationwide Database Search, Felony & Misdemeanor. If the applicant is an alien on a work visa (H1-B/ L1 etc); in such cases international criminal investigations include investigations in applicant's foreign country. Generally the turnaround time to get the national and international criminal report for candidates may take 2-3 weeks.

Drug Screening

Urine sample is taken to investigate and ensure that the candidate is not indulged in drug abuse. Drug results are available usually within 2-5 days after the urine sample is taken from the applicant.

I-9 Compliance / I-9 Verification

The purpose of I-9 compliance is to ensure that employers offer and give employment to persons living in United States lawfully with a valid work authorization only. It is illegal to offer and employ persons who are not authorized to work in US and may attract heave penalty from US government. I-9 form and completing instructions may be downloaded from uscis.gov

"Employers must complete Form I-9 to document verification of the identity and employment authorization of each new employee (both citizen and noncitizen) hired after November 6, 1986, to work in the United States. In the Commonwealth of the Northern Mariana Islands (CNMI), employers must complete Form I-9 to document verification of the identity and employment authorization of each new employee (both citizen and noncitizen) hired after November 27, 2011. Employers should have used Form I-9 CNMI between November 28, 2009 and November 27, 2011

Employers are responsible for completing and retaining Form I-9. For the purpose of completing this form, the term "employer" means all employers, including those recruiters and referrers for a fee who are agricultural associations, agricultural employers, or farm labor contractors Form I-9 is made up of three sections. Employers may be fined if the form is not complete. Employers are responsible for retaining completed forms"
(Reference: http://www.uscis.gov)

Background investigation results

Even if the candidate joins the organization or project and his/her background report does not come clean, employers can terminate the employment immediately. It is unlawful on candidate's part to supply false information knowingly to the employers to seek employment.

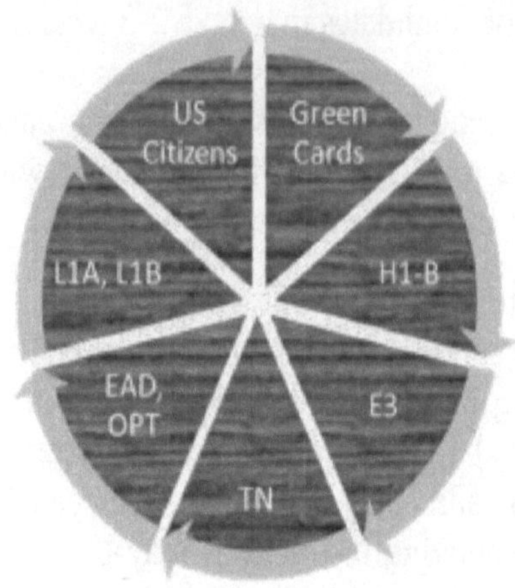

H1-B Visa

The H1-B is a nonimmigrant visa that allows foreign nationals to work in United States temporarily or for specified timeframe in a specialty occupation. Generally H1-B is issued for 3 years and can be extended for additional 3 years. Total duration: 6 Years. H1-B Petitions are accepted by <u>United States Citizenship and Immigration Services</u> (USCIS) from the beginning on April 1 and remain open till the H1-B quota for that year exhausts. In high IT skill demand market, this may be exhausted in 1-2 weeks. The limit is generally 65,000 and additional 20,000. Additional 20,000 quotas is available to foreign nationals holding Masters or higher degree from a US university

Understanding the General Requirements for H1-B Visa

The petitioner (H1-B Petition / Visa sponsor) must be a US employer. Petitioner must establish a valid employer – employee relationship with the potential candidate (beneficiary). Valid employer – employer relation is determined or established by hire and fire rights or the US petitioner (US employer). This includes right to control or supervise the beneficiary.

Specialty occupation: The norm is Bachelor's degree or Higher

Salary / Wages Levels

Potential Candidate (beneficiary) must be paid at least the prevailing wage or higher for the various skill levels. Prevailing Wage Determination (or PWD in short) depends upon the occupation, Skill level and Location / city where the beneficiary will be working. Different occupations have different PWD even at the same location. Additional details on Prevailing Wage Determination and Minimum salary requirements (MSL) can be located at Foreign Labor Certification Data Center website. http://flcdatacenter.com/

H1-B Visa transfer (Normal & Premium processing)

H1-B Transfer Petition (H1B Visa transfer) is required when a person on Valid H1-B visa changes job from one employer to another. NO permission is needed from former employer for the H1B petition transfer.
Under normal processing it may take up to 3 months or even higher for the petition transfer to be approved. Under Premium category, generally the decision is given by 2 weeks after the Transfer Petition is filed with USCIS. If Request for Evidence (RFE) is received then it may take longer even under premium category.
Multiple) H1-B transfer petition can be filed at the same time with more than one employer

What happens if Person Never Travelled to US and holds a Valid H1-B

H1-B Transfer Petition (H1B Visa transfer) can be filed in cap exempt category even if the person never travelled to United States.

Can I work with new employer once Transfer Receipt is received?

Employees can work with the new employer as soon as the Receipt of Petition transfer is received. However it is recommended that employee joins the new employer after the petition transfer (H1B Visa transfer) is approved; Person may become out of status if the petition transfer is denied by USCIS and former employer cancels the H1B visa for the person

General guidelines on Documents Required for H1-B transfer of Petition from Employee

1. Copy of 797 Approval Notice + Copy of previous Visas (if applicable)
2. Copy of resume
3. I 94 Records
4. Copy of Passport
5. Last 3 paystubs
6. Education Certificates: Copy of Degree / Diploma
7. Previous Experience letters
8. Marriage Certificate (Spouse) and Birth Certificate (for Children)
9. Copy of Job Description (Provided by new Employer)
10. Labor Condition Application: LCA ((Provided by new Employer)

Below flowchart explains the H1-B transfer of petition in brief: **Flowchart: H1-B Transfer Petition (H1B Visa transfer)**

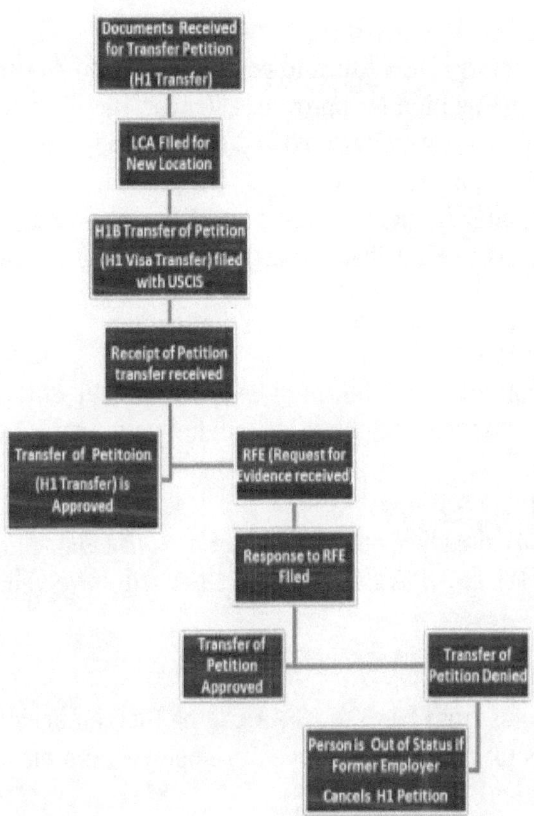

L1 Visa (Intra Company Transfer)

L1 is a nonimmigrant visa available to the employee of international company which has offices at both United States and Foreign country. L1 visa can be classified into L1-A (managerial category) or L1-B

L1-A is a managerial category visa available for for executives and managers. L-1A visa is valid for up to 7 years. L-1B is for employees /workers with specialized knowledge. L1 B visa is valid for 5 years

L1 visa is quota exempt. Spouses of L1 visa get L-2 visa and can get Employment Authorization documents (EAD) to work in United states.

After the completion of 5 years (L1-B) or 7 Years (L1-A)

Change of Status from L1 –B to H1-B

An alien on L1-B visa status in US can find an employer who can sponsor H1B petition and once the petition is approved; alien can file the change of status from L1-B to H1B. Total validity combined for L1B and H1B 6 years; L1B + H1B Total Validity = 6 years

Example if a person has already spent 3.5 years on L1-B visa and adjusts the change of status from L1B to H1B then the new H1-B will have validity of only 2.5 years.

Change of Status from H1-B to L1-A

The change of status from H1-B to L1-A must be approved at least 6 months before the employee reaches maximum 6 years validity period on H1-B visa status

H1-B + L1-A Total Validity = 7 years

Example: if a person has already spent 5 years on H1-B visa and adjusts the change of status from H1B to L1-A then the new L1-A will have validity of only 2 years.

Change of Status from L1-B to L1-A

A petition to change status from L1-B to L1 -A can be filed on behalf of an employee in L1B status to individual to move the employee to a managerial position in the organization.

L1-A + L1-B Total Validity = 7 Years

The change of status from L1-B to L1-A must be approved at least 6 months before the employee reaches maximum 5 years validity period on L1-B visa status

H1-B + L1-A + L1-B Total Validity = 7 Years

Once an Alien has reached the maximum validity, he/ she must spend at least 1 year outside of United States to be eligible to apply for Fresh H1 or L1 visa.

S.No	Item	H1-B	L1-A	L1-B
1	Maximum Validity	6 Years	7 Years	5 Years
2	Quota Exempt	NO	YES	YES
3	LCA & Prevailing Wage Determination needed	YES	NO	NO
4	Dependent Visa	H-4	L2	L2
5	Can Dependent (Spouse) work in US	NO**	YES (L2 EAD)	YES (L2 EAD)
6	Can Employee Change Employer in US	YES	NO	NO
7	Visa Transferable to another employer	YES	NO	NO
8	Bachelor's Degree or Equivalent Required	YES	NO	NO
9	US Salary / Payroll Mandatory	YES	US payroll	US payroll
10	Employee Eligible for Green Card Filing	YES	YES	YES
11	Green Card process: From labor Certification Required	YES	NO	YES
12	Minimum Duration of Employment Required with Sponsoring Company	NO	YES : Minimum 1 year of employment in preceding 3 years with Sponsoring Company	YES : Minimum 1 year of employment in preceding 3 years with Sponsoring Company

Comparison : H1-B, L1-A & L1-B Visa Categories

** Spouses of H1-B visa holders who are on H4 visa are eligible to work in US only if the Green Card application is pending with USCIS for primary H1-B visa holder and his/her I-140 is approved. In such cases, H4 visa holder can apply for Employment Authorization Document (EAD) and can work for any employer in US.

TN Visa / TN Permit

Under The North American Free Trade Agreement (NAFTA); Canadian and Mexican citizens can get a TN Visa / TN permit (TN stands for Treaty National) to work in United States. TN is a Non Immigrant Visa TN visa is valid for 3 years and this can be renewed indefinitely in the multiple of 3 years however TN is a Non Immigrant Visa. If immigration officers detect that TN visa is being used as Green Card then they may deny further extensions. Proof of employment (US offer letter) and Canadian passport is needed for get visa status adjudicated to TN.

Dependents of TN permit holder can get TD permit / Status to enter and stay in US

E3 Visa

E3 is a United States visa available only to the citizens of Australia. E-3 principal applicants must travel to the United States solely to work in a specialty occupation. E3 visa is not available to Permanent Residents of Australia. Spouse of E-3 visa holders may work in the United States without restrictions (unlike H4). E3 Visa is renewable indefinitely in two year increments.

Green Card

Green card or permanent residency is an immigration status which allows a person to stay and work in Unites Statue permanently. Green card is not dependent of any specific employer like H1 or L1 visas. After 5 or more years of good legal standing / status, the green card holder can apply for U.S. citizenship

Green card holders cannot vote in U.S. elections. They cannot remain outside the U.S. for unlimited amounts of time or make their home elsewhere this may result in cancellation of their Green Card and refusal of their request to reenter the United States

US Citizen

Persons born or naturalized in United States. US Citizens are eligible for apply and receive US passport and stay and work in Unites Statue permanently.

Difference between US Citizens and Green Card Holders

S.No	Item	US Citizens	Green Card Holders
1	Voting Rights in US Elections	Available	No Available
2	Eligible to receive a U.S. passport	YES	ONLY Becomes Eligible after 5 years in Lawful GC status
3	Can contest US Elections	YES	No Available
4	Remain outside the U.S. for unlimited amounts of time	YES	NO(GC May be Cancelled)
5	Can be Deported ?	NO	YES
6	Can apply petition (Sponsor) a foreign national family members to join them in the US	YES	NO

F1 Student Employment Options: Practical Training: OPT & CPT for Students on F Visa

OPT is Optional Practical Training; this allows students on F1 in United States to work on a full time basis for one year after they have completed their studies, in a field related to their major.

CPT stands for Curricular Practical Training and allows F1 Students to work for up to 20 hours a week in a field related to their major, while they are engaging in studies. CPT is temporary authorization for practical training directly related to the major field of study for the student.

CPT is intended for the enrolled full-time degree students on the F-1 visa who would like to seek an internship off-campus that relates to their course of study. Their major field of study is listed on their I-20

To complete the I-9 employment verification requirements the following original documents are required:

1. Unexpired Foreign Passport
2. I-94 card stamped F-1 and D/S (Duration of Status), and
3. I-20 form
4. On-Campus Employment Verification Form

Difference between OPT & CPT

CPT is is an integral part of student's curriculum and allows the students to participate in an internship, CPT – student must receive course credit. CPT is employer specific and must be done before students graduate. OPT is optional for any student who meets the eligibility requirements and they don't need to earn academic credit. OPT is not employer specific and may be done before or after you graduate.

Recruiters hiring students on OPT / CPT must ensure the validity of their EAD and comply with I-9 requirements.

H1-B Visa sponsorship for Students on F1 Visa

In addition to annual limit of regular 65,000 numbers, additional 20,000 quotas is available to foreign nationals holding Masters or higher degree from a US university which means foreign national students who complete their master's degree in united states are eligible for this additional H1-B 20,000 quota.

Students must identify an employer who is willing to sponsor their H1-B in 20,000 quotas. The application process and procedure is same as of regular H1-B petitions.

Boolean Operators (Boolean Searches)

AND Boolean Operator

AND logic search will bring results with all the words in the search string. Generally AND logic is used in the resume search on the job boards when 2 or more skills are required in the Job description

Example 1: Search string of Java AND Oracle AND Struts will bring results with candidates who have all 3 key words: Java, Struts and Struts on their resume at least once.

Example 2: Search string of C++ AND Database AND programming AND PMP AND sql will bring results where candidates will have all the key words at least once on their resume: C++ and database and programming and PMP and sql

OR Boolean Operator

OR Boolean search will bring results will at least one of the key words

Example 1: Java OR Oracle OR Struts will bring results with candidates who have at least one of the 3 key words: Java or Struts or Struts on their resume at least once.

Example 2: Search string of C++ OR Database OR programming OR PMP OR sql will bring results where candidates will have ANY ONE of key words at least once on their resume: C++ or database or programming or PMP or sql

NOT Boolean operator

NOT Boolean operator will bring the search results with skill or word will be missing from the search results mentioned after NOT Boolean operator

Example: JAVA NOT C++ will bring the results where resume will contain key word JAVA however the resume will NOT carry C++.

QUOTATION MARKS ""

Using quotation marks will bring results with candidates who have the exact phrase or group of words together.

Example 1: **"Java Developer"** will bring results with resume containing exact phrase "Java Developer"

Example 2: **"Senior Software Architect"** will bring results with resume containing exact phrase in the resume.

Using Parentheses: ( )

Use of Parentheses allows the talent acquisition Professionals to use Boolean search string in multiple ways and in complex search strings. Recruiters can customize their search results more accurately.

Example 1: Search string JAVA AND ORACLE AND ("Project Manager" OR "Project Management") will bring the search results containing key words **Java and Oracle AND Either** "Project Manager" OR "Project Management"

Wild Card Boolean Operators *

Wild Card Boolean Operators or wild card symbol * is used within a word to provide all possible spellings or variations inside a word or word stem

Example 1: Program* will bring the search results Like Programmer, Programming,

Example 2: Comp* will bring the search results with either of these words: Computer Computing, Compensation

Complex search string example:

(JAVA AND ORACLE) AND ("SOFTWARE ENGINEER" OR "COMPUTER ENGINEER") AND (UNIX OR LINUX) AND BANK* AND NOT ("project manager") will bring the search results with key words **JAVA AND ORACLE AND exact phrase of either "SOFTWARE ENGINEER" OR "COMPUTER ENGINEER" AND Either LINUX or Unix AND any of these BANK, BANKING, BANKRUPTCY, BANKER. However the result will not contain the exact phrase "Project Manager"**

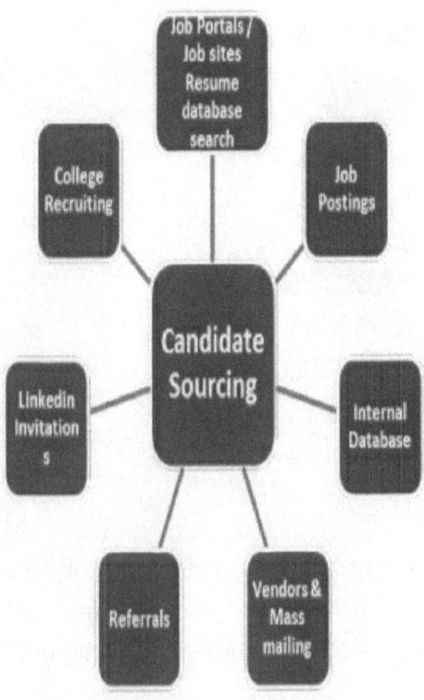

Job Boards / Job websites database resume search

Some of the popular ones are listed below not necessarily in the order of popularity. Active candidates are readily available in resume search section of these website databases. However there are number of candidates who may be active visible on these career sites; however they apply on bob postings which seem relevant to them. It may be a good idea to post the jobs on multiple websites so attract these kinds of job seekers or candidates.

Some of the websites may be flooded by either fake candidate posted by different vendors so recruiters must be cautious when interacting with potential fake or fictions candidates. Best option is to look for local candidates within 20 or 30 miles radius so that you may call them for in person interviews in case of any doubts. Always ask where the candidate currently based at.

Some of the popular US Job Boards:

1. www.dice.com
2. www.monster.com
3. www.careerbuilder.com
4. www.LinkedIn.com
5. www.techfetch.com
6. www.clearancejobs.com
7. www.simplyhired.com
8. www.net-temps.com

Job Postings

Talent acquisition and Staffing professionals must not hurry in job postings on the job boards. Detailed job postings with clear job specifications attract targeted candidates and save recruiters time in filtering our junk or irrelevant applications.

Details like Job city, Zip code, years of experience required, skills & education required, position type (contract, full time), benefits offered if applicable are kind of mandatory for good results.

Vendors and Mass mailing

Mass mailing by either job boards or using a vendor list with email Ids (50s or 100s or ever 1000s of email IDs) can ensure that the requirement reaches maximum number of candidates and vendors. Recruiters should very careful in candidate screening when they receive candidates from these vendors to filter out fake candidates.

Employee Referrals

Employee referrals or candidates referred by existing employees are a powerful tool to source candidates. Since generally the employees know the candidates they are referring to the recruiting teams; recruiters can rely on the referred candidates to some extent.

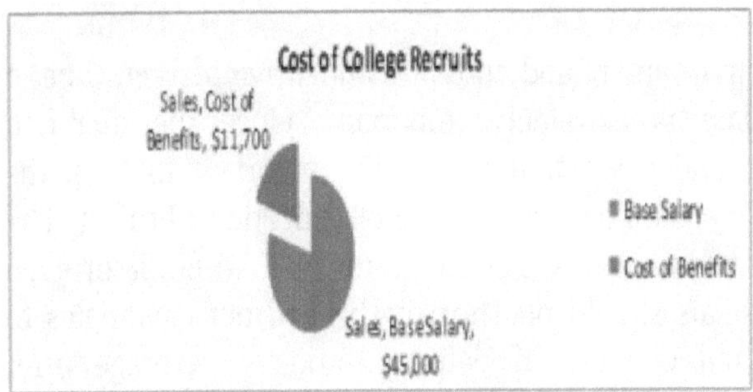

Internal database

Over a period of time; internal database of the company increases and can contain vast number of resumes either active or passive. Reaching out to these candidates increases the recruiters reach to another set of potential candidates.

Visa Ready Candidates in India / Other Countries

Filing suitable number of visa's each year by organizations proactively and transferring employees from overseas on H1 or L1 visa to US is good strategy to source candidates for IT skills not readily available in US market. IT Business leaders plan the visa filing of employees working offshore so that demand of IT skill can be fulfilled by visa ready employee transfers to US in addition to local hiring's

Campus Hiring / Fresher Hiring

Many organizations visit various universities and Colleges; hire fresh graduates and train them to deploy on various projects.

Total Cost: = $45,000/ year Base Salary + $ 11,700 / Year as Cost to Benefits **= $56,700**

Hourly Cost: $56,700 / 1960 = $28.9/Hour. (Without training cost)

It can be very cost effective for organizations to hire college / university fresher's and training them to be deployed on various projects. The the below figure, training costs are not included; even after including the training cost, the overall cost per hour still can be much lower than lateral hire costs

Candidate Sourcing: Turn Around Time & Offer Acceptance Ratios

In the In multi- vendor environment and current competitive market, time to source qualified candidate is extremely important. Once the qualified candidates are identified and offered; it is equally important to keep the offered candidate warm to ensure he/she joins the organization / Project. The best case scenario, offer to join ratios may range for 70% to 80 % or even less. Recruiting Professionals should plan for the backed out candidates to ensure smooth supply and delivery of delivery projects. Average offer acceptance rates may vary for different organizations, it me be above or below the industry averages. Candidates may turn down the offer acceptance for many reasons like better salary package, better benefits, career growth, Location preferences or Band values.

Offer Acceptance Ratio =	Offers Accepted/Offers Extended
Offer Acceptance Ratio =	75 Offers Accepted/100 Offers Extended

In the above example; 75 candidate accepts the offers out of 100 offered candidates, the offer Acceptance Ratio = 75/ 100 = 0.75 or 75 %

US Geography and Time Zones & Daylight Savings

United States has 50 states and primarily 4 time zones across these states. The 4 times zones are:

EST: Eastern Standard Time; CST: Central Standard Time; MST: Mountain Standard Time; PST: Pacific Standard Time. Each time zone lags for 1 hour from previous time zone

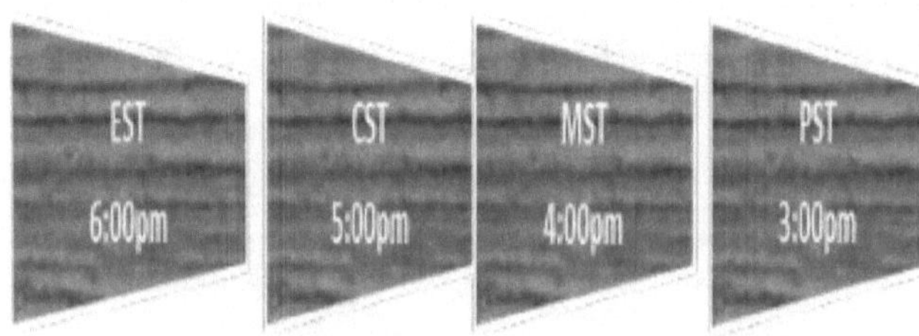

Daylight saving time (DST)

DST is the practice of moving the clocks one hour forward / ahead in summers to utilize the daylight as summers have longer days than winters. In the United States Daylight Saving Time begins at 2:00 am local time on the second Sunday of March. It returns to Standard Time at 2:00 am on the first Sunday in November

50 US States and State Capitals

US State	State Capital	US State	State Capital	US State	State Capital	US State	State Capital
Alabama	Montgomery	Montana	Helena	Iowa	Des Moines	South Carolina	Columbia
Alaska	Juneau	Nebraska	Lincoln	Kansas	Topeka	South Dakota	Pierre
Arizona	Phoenix	Nevada	Carson City	Kentucky	Frankfort	Tennessee	Nashville
Arkansas	Little Rock	New Hampshire	Concord	Louisiana	Baton Rouge	Texas	Austin
California	Sacramento	New Jersey	Trenton	Maine	Augusta	Utah	Salt lake City
Colorado	Denver	New Mexico	Santa Fe	Maryland	Annapolis	Vermont	Montpelier
Connecticut	Hartford	New York	Albany	Massachusetts	Boston	Virginia	Richmond
Delaware	Dover	North Carolina	Raleigh	Michigan	Lansing	Washington	Olympia
Florida	Tallahassee	North Dakota	Bismarck	Minnesota	St. Paul	West Virginia	Charleston
Georgia	Atlanta	Ohio	Columbus	Mississippi	Jackson	Wisconsin	Madison
Hawaii	Honolulu	Oklahoma	Oklahoma City	Missouri	Jefferson City	Wyoming	Cheyenne
Idaho	Boise	Oregon	Salem	Indiana	Indianapolis	Rhode Island	Providence
Illinois	Springfield	Pennsylvania	Harrisburg	50 US States and State Capitals			

Vendor Management System (VMS)

Vendor management system (VMS) is web based (internet) platform that manages contingent workers for clients. Customers can authorize VMS access to their selected or preferred vendors for fulfilling temporary staffing requirements or filling fulltime, permanent positions against defined fees. VMS is an end to end solution which offers not only hiring of contingent workers; however it also manages timesheets, invoice payments and vendor evaluations.

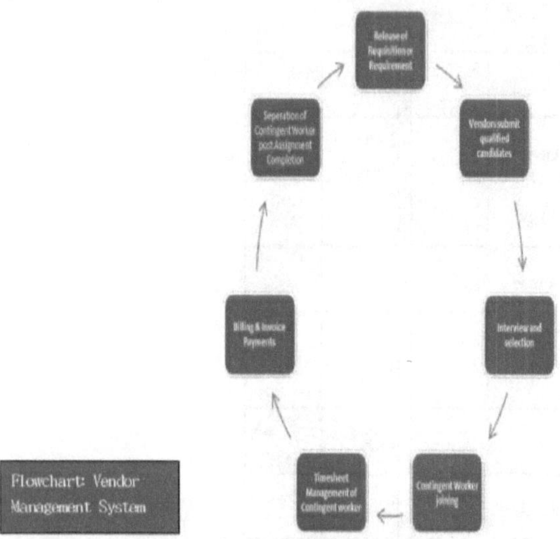

If fair number of vendors are granted access of VMS system by client and number of candidate submittals can be seen by all vendors (without candidate name) then this brings efficiency in the workforce hiring and management. Additionally it also helps in quick turnaround time on resume submittals, interview process and candidate placement. It also allows a healthy competition amongst the vendors to compete for the best qualified resources.

IT Sales & Staff Augmentation

There is clear difference between IT Services sales and Staff Augmentation or selling bodies. IT project sales involve responsibilities more than mere supplying head count to clients. The primary vendor or Tier-1 vendor owns the responsibility of project deliverables cost and timelines. IT sales may be a mix of fixed price, Time and Material (T&M) or Software as a Service (SaaS)

Fixed Bid Contract / Fixed Price Contracts

In Fixed Bid Contract's the owner or Customer agrees to pay a fixed fee or amount for executing a contract or project and customer does not care how will primary vendor pay to their employees or sub vendors. Cost estimation is very important in fixed bid contracts because if the project is not completed on time then it is the responsibility of primary vendor to bear the responsibilities of salaries, wages and sub vendor cost. If cost is estimated in a fair manner considering all the aspects of business; this may give a good profit to the Primary vendors. However if the cost estimation is not correct; the primary vendor may incur losses and they are under contract obligation to finish the project. Quite often there is a penalty fee for delays in the project completion if it deviates from the defined timelines as per the contract.

Time & Material Contracts

In Time & Material Contracts (T&M) the client pays the contractor based on the time (Hours) spent by Contractor's employee, sub- contractors or third party vendors to perform the task or work. T&M contractors are generally used on projects where the requirements most likely change or where the accurate cost estimation of the project / work may not be identified. Most of the W2 contactors, 1099 contractors and Corp to Corp contractors work on T&M business model.

A bigger project may have mix smaller Fixed Bid and T&M projects stitched together. In T&M projects; vendors do not have risk of cost overruns or risks from external environment such as political instability, inflation etc because generally T&M projects have inflation adjusted price hike built in the contract.

Software as a Service (SaaS)

Software as a Service is a software license or Software distribution model in which the applications are hosted by service provider (Vendor) in a central database / computer system. This is also referred to as "on demand" software. The users of SaaS pay a mutually agreed upon fee to the service provider (Vendor) per license. Since SaaS is web based) client- server model; the services provider can host the servers anywhere and provide the services over the internet. Some of the SaaS limitations are data security (data stored on vendor's servers), compatibility and speed (SaaS is cloud based and may not be suitable for services that demand a response time in micro or milliseconds

Farming and Hunting

The Farmer is sales professionals who builds and cultivates the relationships and opportunities, within existing clients, accounts or customers. Farmers are the sales folks who turn a customer from average accounts to great accounts by their relationship and the loyalty they gain from their efforts from the customers. Farmers focus on maintaining long term relationship with customers and "farm" and nurture the existing accounts.

The Hunter is the sales professional who "hunt" for the new opportunity and new customers. It is quite challenging to hunt for new customers. Good Hunters are are independent, focused and target oriented. They are very good in networking skills and building trust with potential clients. Once the hunters win a new account and nurture it well, these new accounts pass on to IT delivery teams and from relationship perspective, they are assigned to "Farmers" or Account managers. Hunters generally have higher sales commission percentage than farmers. You might have heard of Farmer – Hunter role where in addition to account farming, new business development is also expected from farmer-Hunter Professionals. Similarly Hunter-Farmers professionals; in addition to hunting the new clients are expected to farm the new accounts or some of the existing clients

Sales Margin

Margins can be couple of Dollars for layered staff augmentation. You can refer to below diagram which shows the typical margins between layers. It is always recommended to have minimum number of layers or no layers if possible in supply of candidate to achieve greater sales margins.

Example   of   Sales   Margin   in   T&M   Contracts

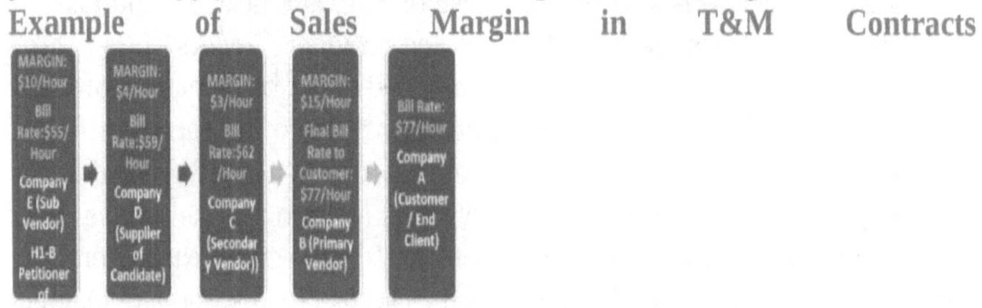

Maintaining the Current Revenues: Challenge for Account Managers

In a given account; it is very important to protect the current revenues and continuously mine the account and help the organization in meeting revenue & sales targets. One challenge in protecting the current revenues is "Attrition" where seasoned and talented employees / Contractors may leave the company and join elsewhere. Therefore HR professionals and business leaders should keep an eye on competition and ensure that the salary and benefits company is offering to employees is in line with the current market forces. Additionally the hourly rate company is offering to contractors is also in sync with the market. It is always a possibility that if the employees / contractors resign and leave the current project, the resource replacement may be offered by competition (another vendor) in onsite environment; resulting in loss of that position and revenue associated with that position. If we look this process on a bigger scale then it is extremely important to control the attrition rates as it directly affects the sales and organization's growth ambitions.

Managing Virtual Employees and Teams

Employees and Contractors working remotely on a project may sometimes feel left out. Including them in all important communications and maintaining constant touch by phone calls, emails and virtual meetings gives them a sense of belonging to the organization. The characteristics of good & productive remote employees also may differ from onsite-in campus employees. Some of the traits of productive remote employees are: self-motivated, disciplined and result oriented.

Bench, IT Sales & Future of US Staff Augmentation

Bench Sales is a sales process at a staffing or recruiting firm to market company's consultants / candidates that are not working on projects/potential client at a given time. Most of these consultants are generally on the staffing agency's payroll. Recruiting firms start marketing their candidates to potential customer when the stipulated project is expected to end in the defined time frame to avoid billing loss or to prevent the consultants to come on actual bench. Staffing companies generally first look for clients requirements and then start to source suitable candidates. However a Bench sales manager has consultants ready to be deployed and they look for clients requirements and supply the consultants on deployable bench.

For IT organizations; it is very important to maintain a healthy bench to ensure that they have some deployable resources at any given point of time and don't rely 100% on external hiring. Positioning internal candidates to Clients has a strategic advantage as internal candidates (employees) are reliable; know the organizational culture and the risk of candidate backouts are illuminated. Maintaining a healthy bench can be a costly affair and it must be in congruence with organizations sales pipeline. Maintaining no bench on 0 % deployable bench can save money in short term; however it is very risky for mid-size to bigger organizations as new projects can run out of qualified resources needed in time and important for project success. It is up to organizations growth appetite to maintain reasonable bench to cater to sales forecasts. Some organizations may maintain up to 10% or higher IT bench Irrespective of business models (Fix bid or T&M or SaaS) organizations that have competency to source qualified candidates in defined time and budget will have clear competitive advantage than competition.

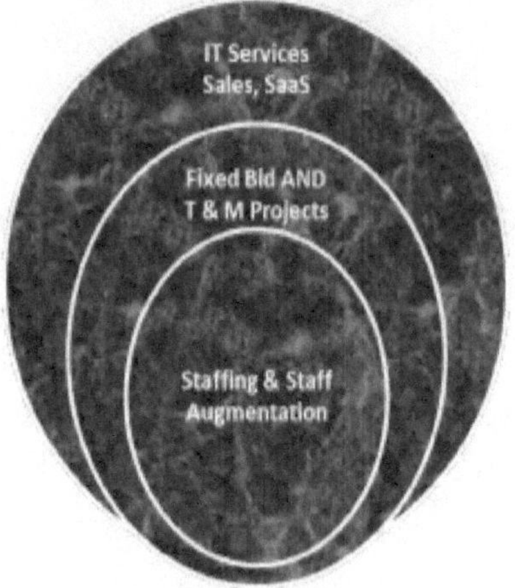

You can see in the above diagram, Staffing and Staff Augmentation is the core of all business models. Accounts grow from small to big by adding resources bit by bit and building blocks of these resources make the account really big. IT Strategy of let the sales team brings the business and then Recruiting teams hire the potential candidates will be a reactive approach in very near future- proactive Approach of Let Sales the teams have leverage of some of good deployable bench to present in front of the customers and additional candidates may be hired upon confirmation from customer after screening of initial lot of candidates.

Bottom-Line

Organizations that have better access to qualified candidates and quicker turnaround time to source candidates have competitive advantage and are more likely to win the Wars of talent and meet their sales targets.

Disclaimer

Any views or opinions presented in this book are solely those of the author and do not necessarily intend to give any legal, immigration or consulting advice. Please consult a professional before making any business decisions based on the fact and figures presented in this book. Readers exempt the author of any legal charges what so ever. Author accepts no liability for the content of this book, or for the consequences of any actions taken on the basis of the information provided, unless that information is subsequently confirmed in writing in addition to professional consultation. Copying, distributing or taking any action on the contents of this book is strictly prohibited.